# Contents

# Introduction

In *Where You've Seen Her,* Grace Bauer gives us a collection of female characters journeying from loneliness and alienation to a rich and many-layered self-acceptance. With humor and a redemptive connection to art and nature, Bauer's unnamed women travel into thickets of disappointing social and intimate relationships. Bauer invites her readers to reflect on the many "selves" within us by showing us the housewife, the princess, the old woman, the junky. Finally, one character speaks of "this face / which wears with / pride or regret / what it has / come through."

In poem after poem, Bauer's female characters tangle with psychological and social realities. One such battle involves the struggle with a patriarchial landscape peopled with male artists and myths about women. Composers and musicians, poets and novelists fill these stanzas and assert their hegemonic power. As Bauer's personae figures begin to articulate other possible realities, the structures (and art forms) begin to break down. Addressing Wallace Stevens in one poem, she declares, "There is no idea of order / here in Key West."

Personifying "Romance" and "Sorrow" as two difficult courtships, Bauer revises the female narrative, thereby thwarting the predictable story for women. In "Her Great Escape," one female character refuses seduction by "Romance," aware that what he's offering is "unreliable as the moon / reflected on the trunk of the Pinto / that's parked down the block." In "Her Steady Date With Sorrow," the feisty female character decides to embrace the companionship which Sorrow offers, thus transforming her loneliness: "At least, she thinks, she'll never lack company. / He's loyal. Consistent." Bauer's free verse stanzas show a careful attention to linebreaks and the musical qualities of language. Occasionally, she surprises her readers by employing formal verse and combining it with a wry humor, as in the skillful and playfully self-mocking villanelle entitled "For Her Villain."

Grace Bauer's project in *Where You've Seen Her* is to examine the process by which we all come to consciousness—within the larger, socially-constructed world. near the middle of the book, in a poem entitled "She Changes Frogs," one character uses fairy tale imagery to focus upon romantic love, a central concern of the collection: "There comes the once upon a time / when the princess / has to ask herself: / is all this worth it / for just one golden ball?" Though Bauer never answers the question directly, her poems show a decided movement towards independence and integration of the many selves within.

Accompanying Bauer's characters on this journey is an intimate experience for the reader. In a poem entitled "His Light Meters. Her Dark Rooms," our narrator states: "there is no beauty / in the subject, as object. . . ." Perhaps this poem is Bauer's "guide" to her understanding of the role of the artist in any culture. Poet or photographer, the artist "makes" a world—selecting, arranging, enlarging—and invites us to enter. *Where You've Seen Her* gives us a world of many narratives; taken together, they tell a multivoiced tale of how we become the subjects of our own stories.

Robin Becker
Cambridge, Massachusetts
March 1993

*"A woman like that is misunderstood.*
*I have been her kind."*

—*Anne Sexton*

## SOMETIMES SHE FEELS LIKE HANK WILLIAMS

Like it's midnight and a train rumbles
by in the distance and she's not poet
enough to think of any word but lonesome.

Hell, she should know a fallacy
when she sees one by now—that train's
got a load, a destination, a deadline.

And she's the one running empty
and so far off track
she can't even carry a tune.

## MORNING BECOMES HER HENRY

She is thumbing the *Dreamsongs*
at three a.m. alarmed
by a silence that keeps her
from falling asleep.
She has no wine, no cigarettes
and no inner resources left.

Lighting fire for water,
she brews some camomile.
Lust and loneliness clench
two fists in the pockets of her
robe as she paces the kitchen.
Even her bones feel bored.

When the kettle whistles, she is
startled into a tension, watching
a woman she never wanted
to know lift a steaming cup
in two hands, settling for
the only warmth she's bound to
get before sunrise.

# SHE CALMS THE SAVAGE BEAST WITH HER AUBADE

Still exhausted at dawn, she plays
Vivaldi, Muddy Waters,
a little Grateful Dead.
She talks to the black rose,
her wandering jew,
the ailing aloe that's yellowed
and rotting from too much attention.

She pinches bits of dill and thyme
for eggs, then remembers
she has none, but she knows
common hunger is not very hard to ignore.

Outside, a wind chime clangs
against a drain pipe, a prism throws
color dancing across white walls.

And the birds, more hungry
than she'll ever feel, peck
the frozen ground before breaking
into what we're used to
calling songs.

# ART LIKE LOVE

She is taking him
at his words.
Pushed to their rough
edges, she leaps
before she looks
into meaning.

Sometimes rhythm
is its own reward.
Sometimes an image
barely glimpsed
is what memory holds
longest.

When she comes across
a perfect line
she lets him take her
inside his poem.

Like a man
inside a woman can
take her
outside of herself.

# HER SEARCH FOR GREAT CAUSES

*Undue Sexual Desire—Causes:*
*Excessive eating of all stimulating foods*
*such as eggs, meats of all kinds, cheese,*
*chocolate, tea, coffee and all alcoholic*
*drinks . . . (novel reading and impure thoughts*
*are also great causes).*

—*Jethro Kloss*

The weather doesn't help much.
Humidity lays its sticky hands
on every inch of skin.
Even the slight stirring
of breeze comes like hot
breath down her neck.

She lies half nude
before an open window
running her tongue around the rim
of a frosted glass of bourbon,
eats oysters—raw
with extra tabasco,
scrapes buttered artichokes
between her perfect white teeth.

Scattered across the rumpled sheets
are D. H. Lawrence, Henry Miller,
Faulkner, a few trashy Gothics.
She has been through the tryst
in the hallway, the corn crib,
that gardener in the grass.
She will wait all of August
for the dark and brooding man,
perhaps a demon, perhaps a wayward heir.
He will sneak up her
stairs in the moonlight
and make her blood run cold.

# HER STEADY DATE WITH SORROW

He shows up like clockwork for three
meals a day, makes her late
for every bus, distracts her on the job.

She comes home to find him drinking
her wine, smoking her last
cigarette, lounging with his boots
propped up on her coffee table.

Oh, he's cocky! He makes himself
right at home. Nights he crowds into bed
between her and her sweetest lovers.

She goes out on the town, trying hard
to lose him, but just as the best
looking man at the bar steps up to ask
her what she's drinking, there's sorrow

that sly devil, peering over his shoulder
and winking to beat the band. After years
of this, she's grown accustomed to him.

At least, she thinks, she'll never lack company.
He's loyal. Consistent. He laughs
at her worst jokes, revises her best lines.

She can count on that bastard.
She knows he'll always be there
whether she needs him or not.

# FOR HER VILLAIN

The time that she wastes missing him is hell,
though no one banks a fire that has grown cold.
And so she thinks she'll write this villanelle.

Though forms are things she doesn't handle well
she thinks that forcing pain into a mold
of verse might help free her from the hell

of missing him. If only she could tell
the truth from all the lies that have been told
and make sense of it in this villanelle

her heart might open like a prison cell
and she might be released from the long hold
he's had on her. Not holding him is hell.

She tries to tell herself it's just as well.
That even if love could be bought and sold
it would cost her more than this cheap villanelle.

In this vignette, she plays the helpless Nell
tied to the tracks or stranded in the cold.
And like a dark-eyed demon straight from hell
he plays the villain. Here's his villanelle.

# ON LSD AT SUNSET PIER SHE THINKS OF WALLACE STEVENS

The orange sunshine drops
through purple haze
into the ocean.
She joins tonight's crowd
in applause.

Sufis dance.
Krishnas chant.
Second-rate musicians
play too loudly.
A queen sways by
with a silver tray, singing
*Don't be shy! Buy my pie!*
*Take a look at my tasty tarts!*

A blue-haired lady on a bike
wheels her poodle around in a basket.
The poodle, in a tartan sweater,
stands on hind legs and points
a little hard-on into the wind.
The mime falls from her invisible ladder.
The juggler drops his balls.

There is no idea of order
here in Key West.
This is all for money and madness.
Anyone singing is singing
for joy or spare change.

# THE VISITING PALEONTOLOGIST FEELS HER THIGH

Home, he is known
as a shy man, given
to minute analysis and quiet
evenings with his family in the den,
but here, he is taken
with the role attention gives him.

She hangs on every word
when he lectures on his digs
in the desert, his theories
of where we've come from
and how far along we've gone.

Afterwards, there are questions
and cocktails. He has too many
of both and by the time
she extends her hand in a simple
greeting, he takes
the gesture for much more
than it's meant; clings to her
slender fingers as if they were
a link he had just uncovered.

He notes the delicate slope
of her cheekbones, the firm
square set of her jaw, but misses
the flash of annoyance
in her eyes when he runs his free hand
down the curve of her spine
and lets it come to rest before
her hipbone as if it belonged.

~

She clears her throat, retreats
across the room to her lover
and wraps her arm around his waist,
hoping the evidence will convince
the man of science she knows
where true affection lies.

He observes the obvious
clues and blushes, then strikes up
a conversation on the Pleistocene Epoch
with a colleague who's eager to please,
and rambles on till the party's over
and she has left without speaking.
By tomorrow, he'll bury the memory
of his embarrassment and her name.
But tonight he sleeps in a stranger's bed
and dreams about the flesh that hides her bones.

# THE MEN ON HER ROOF

She envies them for more
than agility or guts, the view
they're too busy to notice.

It's the fact that they begin
and end, are called upon
by folks like her who need

to keep their feet on firmer ground.
From where she pauses to watch
they appear mechanical

lizard-like, scaling her
walls with their ladders, but she knows
they have a mission

they are sure to accomplish.
Some loose shingle or missing slate
will be back in place, the house secured

against the elements before they quit
and descend; while inside she trudges
her familiar terrain of rugs

and floors—Sisyphus with a vacuum
waging an endless war against her mountain
of proliferating dust. It's not so much

the doing as the fact its never done
that makes a chore of necessary labor.
She knows ordinary lives need space

arranged for order and comfort.
But if beds go unmade for a day
will it keep anyone from dreaming?

Do cobwebs beneath the loveseat
keep anyone out of love?
When the banging above her ceases

she trusts the men have done their work
well and hands them a check
for more than the estimate said

it was likely to cost. They head off
to what she imagines—beer and burgers.
Smoke. A good game of pool.

And she resumes rearranging her den,
pushing the couch into a different
corner. She thinks it opens up

the room—makes it look a little
larger—lets the potted palm
in its wicker cage take in
a little more light.

# SHE THINKS SHE SMELLS A BAD METAPHOR

For years she's worn nothing
but patchouly and musk,
rubbing the earthy oils
between her breasts, behind her ears,
into the crook of her arm
until the sweetness becomes her
signature, lingering
even in the books she has read.

But now she's overwhelmed
with gifts of fragrance:
*Magie Noire* from her mother
*Intimate* from her boss
*White Linen* from her widowed aunt
*Woodhue* from a man who knows she won't.

With so many scents to chose from
she's afraid she'll lose
her own, not recognize the trails
her body leaves her and be left
running round in circles, barking
up a tree that holds no game.

Even the faithful dog
she's fed for years will
sniff her crotch and whine
at the unfamiliar redolence of *Heaven Scent*
or *Charles of the Ritz*.

She knows she is no *Xanadu*.
No *Opium*. No *Obsession*.

At night her lover tells
her she's raw
oysters and honey. In the morning
she tastes *L'air du Temps* on his tongue.

# SHE CHANGES FROGS

It is not always a kiss
that transforms him.
In fact, in one version
she has to knock him up
against a wall
to achieve the desired result.

Some point to her change of heart
and declare: *Another fickle woman*!
But his cold-blooded manner
would have forced the noblest love
to some strange end.

All that croaking
at the dinner table,
the swamp mud on her royal lap
and the slime in her canopied bed.
Not to mention her daddy, the king,
always lecturing on promises
as if he'd never broken
one in his life.

There comes the once upon a time
when the princess
has to ask herself:
is all this worth it
for just one golden ball?

## THE SLEEP WALKER DREAMS HER WAKENING

She's been asleep
so long
she no longer
recalls

if she dreamed
the dream
or it dreamed
her

fallen
in love
with a pain
that allows no

feeling
a daze
that lets her
watch

the world performed
like a play
behind a scrim
of gauze

and she
need not
pay
attention

until the final
act
when she runs
down

~

all those tracks
    she's laid
            head on
into

a crash
    that always comes
and lays her
    out

in a cold
    sweat
            her eyes
vacant

and dark
    as blackened spoons
            as she suffers
the light

watches the dream
    collapse
        like any vein
hit

once too often.

# HER HAPPILY EVER AFTER

His father told him
*Never trust a woman, son,*
*especially a pretty one.*
So he never does

though he marries a girl
who is lovely, and true
as a woman can be to someone
other than herself.

He buys her a house he likes.
He doubts every word she speaks.
He tells a few lies of his own
just in case, or in spite.

She never complains or understands.
She tends a garden of herbs.
She works elaborate needlepoints,
cooks his favorite meals.

Years pass this way.
Small talk gives in to silence.
They age; her beauty fades.
Still he thinks she might prove false.

The warning hangs like a tapestry
between them; neither remembers
ever caring. Her stitches grow

finer and finer.
He drinks. No one recalls
their once upon a time.

# HER GREAT ESCAPE

Romance pulls in
to her driveway in a grey car.
Their hands reach for warmth
across the gear shift
as they talk themselves deeper
into the desire they are
trying to talk themselves out of.

The moon's a white slice
in a black sky, like the moons
that tip their twined fingers,
like the Cheshire cat's
half-assed smile,
like all the cheesy similes
she has heard the moon be like.

She'd hand over her credit card
if she thought he'd drive
her anywhere but crazy.
Pay for all the gas.
But what he's offering is temperate
as the climate, unreliable as the moon
reflected on the trunk of the Pinto
that's parked down the block.

Smooth as Sam Cooke
singing *You Send Me* on the radio,
she bows out on the last refrain
and leaves what might be
possible, idling in the dark.

# SHE MARVELS AT HIS FACE

which appears in dreams still
so clear after all these years—
clearer than the sky which,
this morning, is lost
in a haze; clearer than the face
of the man who, last night
in the pale blue light of a bar,
mistook her for a woman he claimed
he once knew in Chicago.
He seemed so sure and happy.
She thought she might be
better off as that woman
who could inspire so much delight
by a chance reappearance.
For a moment, the wind and the blues
of a city she'd never even seen
became her past, till her mid-western
friend turned back to his bourbon
and said, *No, I guess you're too tall*
*and too young, and it's better*
*you're not her after all these years.*
She repeats the words: *after all these years* . . .
as if it were the first time she'd heard
them, and wonders why *these*
is so important? Why *these* negates
all the years that came before, when the face
that might have been hers
in a bar or his in a dream
was a sight beyond question—
too familiar to notice, too constant
to miss or imagine ever gone.
She thinks maybe memory has it all
wrong—his lips were thinner,
his eyes a duller brown
and she's really smaller
than she appears. Still a girl
despite time. After all,
these years have a way
of deceiving us with the burden
of whatever we've gained in them,
the blindness of all weve lost.

## SHE HAS DAYS

she walks through wondering
  what it would be like

to be someone, anyone
  other than who she is:
    the woman at the market

wheeling a cart piled
  with Pampers and beer
    the housewife in a blue

plaid dress bending
  over a new bed
    of geraniums, coaxing

color from poor soil
  the hard-hatted woman
    on Main Street behind

the MEN WORKING sign, stopping
  the flow of traffic with a wave
    of her strong, slender hand

the girl crouched on her porch swing
  painting her toenails
    pink—the very image

of concentration. It might
  have something to do with
    choices, but she can't recall

ever having chosen to be
  what she is, where
    she's at at this moment

only choosing to sleep
  late some mornings, to rise
    before dawn others—and even

this seemed more a force
  than choice, something urging
    her into or out of dreams

~

for no good reason, just to watch
  light play as it will across
    sky, through dust

on windows, choosing to wear
  one dress instead of another
    to turn left on the road

where a doe stands frightened
  transfixed by the lights of her car
    choosing to turn the lights off

and watch her shadow bound
  into a thicket, choosing
    to reply yes or no to a question

without thinking and then
  having to live with the answer
    and think about why she ever

had to give it. But what does this
  have to do with today when the sky
    divides like a palette into shades

of gray it's hard not to see
  as a projection of her own
    mood, some split inside her

between darkness and another
  kind of darkness which lies
    just the other side of a light

strong enough to blind anyone
  who chooses to stare straight
    into it, squinting at the familiar

figure who wanders toward her
  in the market offering a choice
    piece of fruit, at the nursery

bearing seedlings in a plastic
  flat, wearing the sleek blue
    dress she decided to put on

this morning of her
  life on this green earth.

# HER NEW BIRDS

All winter she has watched
them through the window:
one red-breasted woodpecker
two tufted titmice, half a dozen
mourning doves and more

slate-colored junkos than she ever
managed to count. Not to mention
a varied slew of sparrows, the jays
who got so fat and comfortable
they took to preening on the porch

not bothering to retreat
when she got close. She liked to think
she'd earned their trust, maybe
even friendship, but today they're gone
and a flock of strange starlings

run rampant on the grass, bold
enough to attack a lone
squirrel—who has come, she supposes,
out of his seasonal hiding—
and squawk at her as she approaches

with fresh seed, as if to warn
her away from what's theirs.
*Ungrateful*, she thinks, *they'd bite*
*the hand that feeds them.*
Still, she does. Hoping

the sun that catches
rainbows on their stark
wings signals spring will soon
be coming—no matter what else
may be forced to leave.

# HIS LIGHT METERS. HER DARK ROOMS.

### 1. The Photographer Explains His Poor Exposure

The problem with the photo
is I left my shutter
too wide open for too long,
absorbed too much
surrounding light.
Her image got lost in the glare.

I should have realized
from the contact sheets
all the fixer in the world
would never capture what I had
seen clearly, but I tried
to develop it over and over,
hoping I could make her
come out of the negative.

### 2. The Man Behind Her Picture

He labors through the night
in his tiny room
which guarantees
the darkness he needs

enlarging gestures
she never would have
noticed, cropping what he
calls *distracting details*
to compose her
into perfect still life.

But her best moments
are more cinematic.
Each one flashes
by so rapidly, she appears
to be going somewhere.

~

### 3. Alone In the Gallery

She is the only mobile figure
in the room, framed
by faces staring
from the walls.

The light is bad.
She must side-step
each portrait
to avoid seeing
her own features
reflected in the glass.

As she walks from print
to print, she imagines
still eyes imagining her
caught in a moment
and framed behind glass
in an empty room.

### 4. On Seeing Herself In The Show

It could be anyone's shoulder.
But he points out the particulars
of hair, chin, breasts—
angles and arcs he found
worth attention, if only for shadows
they happened to cast at the time.

Though there is no beauty
in the subject, as object
she forms a composition of interest.
Anonymous in the beholder's eye.
A lovely lie of light.

# SHE DOESN'T KNOW

what to make
  of these lines

that invade her
  face like boundaries
    on a map

she's never learned
  how to read
    Laughter pain

or mere weather
  the sun or wind
    she welcomed in

an earlier life
  whatever the cause
    the body ignores

it forms memories
  to a sort
    of lingering scar

that testifies life
  has been lived
    through in this

body this face
  which wears with
    pride or regret

what it has
  come through been
    touched by   Endured.

# WHERE YOU'VE SEEN HER

After Cindy Sherman

Perhaps you caught her gazing
  at her image in a mirror, or staring
out a window into a distance you thought
  might be yours. Perhaps you saw yourself
in her eyes.

Perhaps it was in moonlight or starlight,
  in the blue haze of a t.v. screen or
the smoke of a seedy bar where the glow
  from her cigarette gathered the night
around; or perhaps it was in sunlight
  so bright

you had to squint. It hurt
  your eyes. Maybe you've never seen
her at all, or so often you have long
  since forgotten to look, allowing
memory or expectation to make what you think
she is real.

Perhaps you've brushed by her
  in a subway, at a close-out sale,
in some library where she reached
  for the very book you wanted to read;
or maybe in a dream she cruised by
  in a red

sedan, on a black mare, saying something
  you couldn't quite fit your voice
around, but desperately needed to say.
  She could be your mother, your sister,
your favorite or most hated aunt,
  the girl

~

next door, the one you left
  behind, who got away, the woman too
good or not good enough for you, the one
  who never knew you existed, who's been
waiting for you all her life, the one
  you've been

mistaken for. Perhaps you gave her
  your ring, took her cherry, paid
for her lunch, lent her cabfare
  or lipstick, voted her *Snow Queen*
or *Most Congenial*. You might have
  given her

flowers, advice, or hell,
  a lift to the nearest phone booth,
the time of day. You might have opened
  doors for her, or old wounds,
maybe you held her or wished you could
  hold her

or be her or never had been.
  She is always more or less
than you imagined or would have
  her be. She is the stranger you
always recognize. More than shadow
  less than

substance, not quite yours or her own.
  Since she has never really been
there, you know that she can never
  go away.

To Order These Other Titles in the **Pennywhistle** Chapbook Series, Contact:

PENNYWHISTLE PRESS
P.O. BOX 734
TESUQUE, NEW MEXICO, 87574
Telephone: (505) 982-2622
Fax Orders: (505) 982-6858

**What Makes A Woman Beautiful** by Joan Logghe
Introduction by Jim Sagel, ISBN 0-938631-15-2 $ 6.00

**Decoy's Desire** by Kerry Shawn Keys
Introduction by Gerald Stern, ISBN 0-938631-14-4 $6.00

**Where You've Seen** Her by Grace Bauer
Introduction by Robin Becker, ISBN 0-938631-11-X $6.00

**Still the Sirens** by Dennis Brutus
Introduction by Lamont B. Steptoe, ISBN 0-938631-09-8 $ 6.00

**Portal** by Joyce Jenkins
Introduction by Carolyn Kizer, ISBN 0-938631-18-7 $6.00

**No Golden Gate for Us** by Francisco X. Alarcón
Introduction by Juan Felipe Herrera, ISBN 0-938631-16-0 $6.00

**Tesuque Poems** by Victor di Suvero
Introduction by Pierre Delattre, ISBN 0-938631-17-9 $6.00

**Further Sightings & Conversations** by Jerome Rothenberg
Introduction by Michael Palmer, ISBN 0-938631-09-9 $5.00

**Who is Alice?** by Phyllis Stowell
Introduction by Sandra Gilbert, ISBN 0-938631-04-7 $5.00

**The Sum Complexities of the Humble Field** by Viola Weinberg
Introduction by Mary Mackey, ISBN 0-938631-06-3 $5.00

**Sublunary** by Jorge H.-Aigla
Introduction by Charles G. Bell, ISBN 0-938631-07-1 $5.00

**The Width of a Vibrato** by Edith A. Jenkins
Introduction by Robert Glück, ISBN 0-938631-10-1 $5.00

**The Fields** by Richard Silberg
Introduction by Joyce Jenkins, ISBN 0-938631-05-5 $5.00

**Full Turn** by Sarah Blake
Introduction by Dorianne Laux, ISBN 0-938631-08-X $5.00

**Hardwired for Love** by Judyth Hill
Introduction by Miriam Sagan, ISBN 0-938631-13-6 $5.00

**Falling Short of Heaven** by Suzanne Lummis
Introduction by Austin Strauss, ISBN 0-938631-12-8 $5.00